Way o

with
Pope Benedict XVI

Meditations and Prayers by
His Most Reverend Eminence
Card. Joseph Zen Ze-Kiun, S.D.B.
Bishop Of Hong Kong

*All booklets are published thanks to the
generous support of the members of the
Catholic Truth Society*

CATHOLIC TRUTH SOCIETY
PUBLISHERS TO THE HOLY SEE

Contents

Presentation

... Clearly, the central figure in this *Via Dolorosa* is Our Lord Jesus Christ, as he is presented to us by the Gospels and the Church's tradition. Yet behind him there are many people from the past and the present, including ourselves. In our prayer let us be mindful of the presence of so many brothers and sisters from times past. They, probably more than ourselves, experienced in their bodies the Passion of Jesus. In their flesh, Jesus was newly arrested, maligned, tortured, derided, dragged and crushed under the weight of the Cross, and nailed to that wood like a criminal.

Obviously, we are not alone at the Colosseum. Present in the Holy Father's heart and in our own hearts are all the "living martyrs" of the 21st century. *Te martyrum candidatus laudat exercitus.*

When we think of persecution, let us also remember the persecutors. As I was drafting the text of these meditations, it frightened me to realise how unchristian I am. I had to make a great effort to purify myself of uncharitable sentiments towards those who caused Jesus to suffer and those who are causing our brothers and sisters to suffer in the world today. Only when I confronted my sins and my own lack of faithfulness, did I succeed in seeing myself among the persecutors, and then I was moved to repentance and gratitude for the forgiveness of our merciful Master.

So let us now begin our meditation, let us sing and pray to Jesus and with Jesus for those who suffer on account of his Name, for those who cause him and his brothers and sisters to suffer, and for ourselves, who are sinners and at times also his persecutors.

Opening Prayer

In the name of the Father, and of the Son, and of the Holy Spirit.
R. Amen.

Jesus our Saviour,
we are gathered here on this day, at this hour and in this place, remembering your many servants who were torn to pieces and killed here, centuries ago, amid the roars of the hungry lions and the cries of the spectators, for their faithfulness to your Name.

Today, we come here to express to you the gratitude of your Church for the gift of salvation won by your Passion.

Colosseums have multiplied down the centuries, wherever our brothers and sisters in different parts of the world continue to be harshly persecuted today, prolonging your Passion. Together with you and our persecuted brothers and sisters around the world, we begin this journey along the *Via Dolorosa* with deep emotion, the journey that you once travelled with such great love.

Way of the Cross - 20th Century
Society of the Divine Word Generalate Archives - Rome

First Station

Jesus in agony in the Garden of Olives

V. *(genuflecting)* We adore you, O Christ and praise you.
R. Because by Your Holy Cross you have redeemed the world.

From the Gospel according to Mark 14:2-36

And they went to a place which was called Gethsemane; and Jesus said to his disciples, "Sit here, while I pray." And he took with him Peter and James and John, and began to be greatly distressed and troubled. And he said to them, "My soul is very sorrowful, even to death; remain here, and watch." And going a little farther, he fell on the ground and prayed that, if it were possible, the hour might pass from him. And he said, "Abba, Father, to you all things are possible; remove this cup from me; yet not what I will, but what you will."

Meditation

Jesus experienced fear, anguish and sorrow, even to death. He took with him three companions, but soon they fell asleep, and he began to pray alone: "May this hour pass from me, take away this chalice from me... Yet, Father, may your will be done."

He had come into the world in order to do the Father's will, but never before had he tasted the full depth of the bitterness of sin, or felt so helpless.

In his Letter to the Catholics in China, Benedict XVI recalled the vision in the Apocalypse of St John where the apostle weeps before the sealed book of human history, the *mysterium iniquitatis*.

Only the Lamb that was slain is capable of removing the seal. In many parts of the world, the Bride of Christ is undergoing the dark hour of persecution, as Esther once did when threatened by Haman, as did the "Woman" of the Apocalypse when threatened by the dragon. Let us be watchful, and let us accompany the Bride of Christ in our prayer.

Prayer

Jesus, Almighty God, you chose to become weakness because of our sins, you recognise the cries of the persecuted, which are the echo of your agony. They ask: Why this oppression? Why this humiliation? Why this prolonged servitude?

The words of the Psalm come to mind: "Awake, Lord, why do you sleep? Awake! Do not cast us off for ever! Why do you hide your face, why do you forget our affliction and oppression? For we lie prostrate in the dust, our body cleaves to the ground. Rise up, come to our help!" (*Ps* 43.24-26).

No, Lord! You did not have recourse to this Psalm in Gethsemane, but you said: "Your will be done!"

You could have summoned twelve legions of angels, but you did not. Lord, suffering makes us afraid. We are tempted once again to grasp at easy means of success. Help us not to be afraid of fear, help us to trust in you.

All:
Our Father, who art in heaven,
hallowed be thy name.
Thy Kingdom come.
Thy will be done on earth as it is in heaven.
Give us this day our daily bread,
and forgive us our trespasses,
as we forgive those who trespass against us,
and lead us not into temptation,
but deliver us from evil.

At the Cross her station keeping,
Stood the mournful Mother weeping,
Close to Jesus to the last.

Way of the Cross - 20th Century
Society of the Divine Word Generalate Archives - Rome

Second Station

Jesus is betrayed by Judas
and abandoned by his disciples

V. *(genuflecting)* We adore you, O Christ and praise you.
R. Because by Your Holy Cross you have redeemed
the world.

From the Gospel according to Mark 14:43a, 45-46, 50-52

*And immediately, while Jesus was still speaking, Judas
came, one of the Twelve. And he went up to Jesus at once
and said, "Master!" And he kissed him. And they laid
hands on him and seized him. And the disciples all forsook
him and fled. And a young man followed him, with nothing
but a linen cloth about his body; and they seized him, but
he left the linen cloth and ran away naked.*

Meditation

Betrayal and abandonment on the part of those he had
chosen as Apostles, those he had entrusted with the
secrets of the Kingdom, those he had trusted completely!
Total failure, then. What sorrow, what humiliation!

Yet all this took place to fulfil the sayings of the
prophets. Otherwise, how could the ugliness of sin have
been exposed, which is simply the betrayal of love?

Betrayal causes surprise, especially if it even involves the shepherds of the flock. How could they do this to him? The spirit is strong, but the flesh is weak. Temptations, threats and blackmail bend the will. Yet, what a scandal! What great sorrow in the Lord's heart!

Let us not be scandalised! Defections are never lacking at times of persecution. And afterwards, people have often returned to the fold. In that young man who cast away the linen cloth and ran away naked (cf. *Mk* 14:51-52), authoritative interpreters have seen the future evangelist Mark.

Prayer

Lord, those who flee from your Passion are left without dignity. Have mercy on us, who stand naked before your Majesty. Let us place before you our most shameful wounds.

Jesus, to abandon you is to abandon the sun. If we seek to rid ourselves of the sun, we fall back into cold and darkness.

Father, we have distanced ourselves from your house. We are not worthy to be received back by you. Yet you have given orders that we should be washed and robed, supplied with sandals and a ring on our finger.

All:

Our Father, who art in heaven,
hallowed be thy name.
Thy Kingdom come.
Thy will be done on earth as it is in heaven.
Give us this day our daily bread,
and forgive us our trespasses,
as we forgive those who trespass against us,
and lead us not into temptation,
but deliver us from evil.

Through her heart His sorrow sharing,
All His bitter anguish bearing,
Now at length the sword has passed.

Way of the Cross - 20th Century
Society of the Divine Word Generalate Archives - Rome

Third Station

Jesus is condemned by the Sanhedrin

V. *(genuflecting)* We adore you, O Christ and praise you.
R. Because by Your Holy Cross you have redeemed the world.

From the Gospel according to Mark 14:55, 61b-62a, 64b

Now the chief priests and the whole council sought testimony against Jesus to put him to death; but they found none. The high priest asked him, "Are you the Christ, the Son of the Blessed?" And Jesus said, "I am!" And they all condemned him as deserving death.

Meditation

The Sanhedrin was the court of justice of God's people. Now this court condemns Christ, the Son of the Blessed One, and judges him to be deserving of death.

The Innocent One is condemned "because he has blasphemed," say the judges, and they tear their garments. Yet we know from the Evangelist that they did so through envy and hatred.

St John says that ultimately the high priest had spoken in God's Name: only by allowing his innocent Son to be condemned could God the Father save the guilty brothers of Jesus.

Across the centuries, hosts of innocent people have been condemned to atrocious sufferings. Some cry out against the injustice, but it is they, the innocent, who, in communion with Christ, the Innocent One, atone for the sins of the world.

Prayer

Jesus, you are not concerned to prove your innocence, you are solely intent upon restoring to man the righteousness that he lost through sin.

We were your enemies, there was no way for us to change our condition. You let yourself be condemned in order to grant us forgiveness. Saviour, help us to avoid bringing condemnation upon ourselves on the last day. *Iudex ergo cum sedebit, quicquid latet apparebit; nil inultum remanebit. Iuste iudex ultionis, donum fac remissionis ante diem rationis.*

All:

Our Father, who art in heaven,
hallowed be thy name.
Thy Kingdom come.
Thy will be done on earth as it is in heaven.
Give us this day our daily bread,
and forgive us our trespasses,
as we forgive those who trespass against us,
and lead us not into temptation,
but deliver us from evil.

Oh, how sad and more distressed
Was that Mother highly blessed
Of the sole-begotten One!

Way of the Cross - 20th Century
Society of the Divine Word Generalate Archives - Rome

Fourth Station

Jesus is denied by Peter

V. *(genuflecting)* We adore you, O Christ and praise you.
R. Because by Your Holy Cross you have redeemed the world.

From the Gospel according to Mark 14:66-68, 72

And as Peter was below in the courtyard, one of the maids of the high priest came; and seeing Peter warming himself, she looked at him and said, "You also were with the Nazarene, Jesus." But he denied it, saying, "I neither know nor understand what you mean." And immediately the cock crowed a second time. And Peter remembered how Jesus had said to him, "Before the cock crows twice, you will deny me three times." And he broke down and wept.

Meditation

"Even if I must die with you, I will not deny you" (*Mk* 14:31). Peter was sincere when he said this, but he did not know himself, he did not know his own weakness. He was generous, but he had forgotten that he needed the generosity of the Master. He claimed he would die for Jesus, but it was Jesus who was to die for him, to save him.

In making Simon the "rock" on which to build his Church, Christ involved the Apostle in his initiative of salvation. Peter naively believed that he could give something to the Master, but instead, everything was freely given to him by Christ, including forgiveness after his denial.

Jesus did not withdraw his choice of Peter as the foundation of his Church. After repenting, Peter was given the capacity to strengthen his brethren.

Prayer

Lord, when Peter speaks, enlightened by the Father's revelation, he acknowledges you as the Christ, the Son of the living God. When, on the other hand, he trusts his own reason and good will, he becomes an obstacle to your mission. Presumption causes him to deny you, his Master, while humble repentance confirms him once more as the rock on which you build your Church. Your choice to entrust the continuation of the work of salvation to weak and vulnerable men manifests your wisdom and power.

Protect the men you have chosen, Lord, so that the gates of the underworld will never prevail against your servants.

Direct your gaze upon all of us, as you did that night upon Peter after the cock crowed.

All:

Our Father, who art in heaven,
hallowed be thy name.
Thy Kingdom come.
Thy will be done on earth as it is in heaven.
Give us this day our daily bread,
and forgive us our trespasses,
as we forgive those who trespass against us,
and lead us not into temptation,
but deliver us from evil.

Christ above in torments hangs;
She beneath beholds the pangs
Of her dying glorious Son.

Way of the Cross - 20th Century
Society of the Divine Word Generalate Archives - Rome

Fifth Station

Jesus is judged by Pilate

V. *(genuflecting)* We adore you, O Christ and praise you.
R. Because by Your Holy Cross you have redeemed the world.

From the Gospel according to Mark 15:12-15

And Pilate again said to them, "Then what shall I do with the man whom you call the King of the Jews?" And they cried out, "Crucify him." And Pilate said to them, "Why, what evil has he done?" But they shouted all the more, "Crucify him." So Pilate, wishing to satisfy the crowd, released for them Barabbas; and having scourged Jesus, he delivered him to be crucified.

Meditation

Pilate appeared powerful, he was in a position to determine the life or death of Jesus. He enjoyed that ironic reference to the "King of the Jews", but in truth he was weak, wretched and servile. He was afraid of the Emperor Tiberius, he was afraid of the people, he was afraid of the chief priests, while nevertheless despising them in his heart. He handed Jesus over to be crucified, knowing that he was innocent.

In his vain attempt to save Jesus, he ended up granting freedom to a dangerous murderer.

To no avail he sought to wash those hands, dripping with innocent blood.

Pilate is the image of all those who wield authority as an instrument of power, having no regard for justice.

Prayer

Jesus, through your courage in declaring yourself king, you sought to awaken Pilate to the voice of his conscience. Enlighten the consciences of the many people in positions of authority, so that they may recognise the innocence of your followers. Give them the courage to respect religious freedom.

The temptation to cultivate the powerful and oppress the weak is very widespread. And the powerful are those who wield authority, those who control trade and the mass media; but there are also people who allow themselves to be easily manipulated by the powerful into oppressing the weak. How could those people cry out "Crucify him!" after they had known you as a compassionate friend, one who had only ever done good to everyone?

All:

Our Father, who art in heaven,
hallowed be thy name.
Thy Kingdom come.
Thy will be done on earth as it is in heaven.
Give us this day our daily bread,
and forgive us our trespasses,
as we forgive those who trespass against us,
and lead us not into temptation,
but deliver us from evil.

Is there one who would not weep,
Whelmed in miseries so deep,
Christ's dear Mother to behold?

Way of the Cross - 20th Century
Society of the Divine Word Generalate Archives - Rome

Sixth Station

Jesus is scourged and crowned with thorns

V. *(genuflecting)* We adore you, O Christ and praise you.
R. Because by Your Holy Cross you have redeemed the world.

From the Gospel according to Mark 15:15b, 17-19

Pilate, having scourged Jesus, delivered him to be crucified. Then the soldiers clothed him in a purple cloak, and plaiting a crown of thorns they put it on him. And they began to salute him, "Hail, King of the Jews!" And they struck his head with a reed and spat upon him, and they knelt down in homage to him.

Meditation

Scourging as it was practised in those days was a terrible punishment. The dreadful flagellum used by the Romans tore the flesh to shreds. And the crown of thorns, apart from causing the most acute pain, was also a mockery of the divine prisoner's kingship, as were the spitting and the blows.

Appalling forms of torture continue to emerge from the cruelty of the human heart - and psychological tortures are no less terrible than the physical variety; often the victims themselves become torturers in their turn. Are all these sufferings meaningless?

Prayer

No, Jesus, you continue to gather together and sanctify suffering of all kinds: that of the sick, of those who die in hardship, of all who experience discrimination; but the sufferings which shine out over all others are those endured for your Name.

By the sufferings of the martyrs, bless your Church; may their blood become the seed of new Christians. We firmly believe that their sufferings, even if at the time they seem like total defeat, will bring true victory to your Church. Lord, grant constancy to our persecuted brethren!

All:
Our Father, who art in heaven,
hallowed be thy name.
Thy Kingdom come.
Thy will be done on earth as it is in heaven.
Give us this day our daily bread,
and forgive us our trespasses,
as we forgive those who trespass against us,
and lead us not into temptation,
but deliver us from evil.

Bruised, derided, cursed, defiled,
She behold her tender Child,
All with bloody scourges rent.

Way of the Cross - 20th Century
Society of the Divine Word Generalate Archives - Rome

Seventh Station

The Cross is placed upon Jesus' shoulders

V. *(genuflecting)* We adore you, O Christ and praise you.
R. Because by Your Holy Cross you have redeemed the world.

From the Gospel according to Mark 15:20

And when they had mocked him, they stripped him of the purple cloak, and put his own clothes on him. And they led him out to crucify him.

Meditation

The Cross, that great symbol of Christianity, from being an instrument of shameful punishment has become a glorious victory banner.

There are courageous atheists who are ready to sacrifice themselves for the revolution: they are prepared to embrace the cross, but without Jesus.

Among Christians there are *de facto* "atheists" who want Jesus, but without the Cross. Now without Jesus, the cross is unbearable, and without the Cross, no one can claim to be with Jesus. Let us embrace the Cross and let us embrace Jesus, and with Jesus let us embrace all our suffering and persecuted brethren!

Prayer

O divine Redeemer, with what great joy you embraced the Cross, which you had desired for so long! It weighs heavily upon your wounded shoulders, but it is held up by a heart filled with love.

The great Saints understood the saving value of the Cross so deeply that they could cry out: "Either suffer or die!" Give us the grace at least to accept your invitation to carry our cross behind you. You prepared a personal cross for each one of us. We have before our eyes the image of Pope John Paul II, who climbed the Mount of Crosses in Lithuania. Every one of those crosses had a story to tell, a story of suffering and joy, of humiliation and triumph, of death and resurrection.

All:
Our Father, who art in heaven,
hallowed be thy name.
Thy Kingdom come.
Thy will be done on earth as it is in heaven.
Give us this day our daily bread,
and forgive us our trespasses,
as we forgive those who trespass against us,
and lead us not into temptation,
but deliver us from evil.

Can the human heart refrain,
From partaking in her pain,
In that Mother's pain untold?

Way of the Cross - 20th Century
Society of the Divine Word Generalate Archives - Rome

Eighth Station

Jesus is helped by Simon of Cyrene to carry the Cross

V. *(genuflecting)* We adore you, O Christ and praise you.
R. Because by Your Holy Cross you have redeemed the world.

From the Gospel according to Mark 15:21

And they compelled a passer-by, Simon of Cyrene, who was coming in from the country, the father of Alexander and Rufus, to carry his Cross.

Meditation

Simon of Cyrene was coming in from the country. He stumbled upon the procession of death and was pressed into carrying the Cross together with Jesus.

At a later date, he confirmed this act of service, expressing his satisfaction at having been of assistance to the poor condemned prisoner, and he became one of the disciples in the early Church. He was surely the object of admiration and even envy for the special privilege of having comforted Jesus in his sufferings.

Prayer

Dear Jesus, you would have thanked Simon of Cyrene for his help, even though the Cross was actually owed to him and to each one of us. In this way, Jesus, you are grateful to us every time we help our brothers and sisters to carry their cross, although we are simply doing our duty in order to atone for our sins.

Jesus, you are at the origin of this cycle of compassion. You bear our cross, thereby enabling us to assist you in your brothers and sisters to carry the cross.

Lord, as members of your Body, we help one another to carry the cross, and we admire the great throng of "Simons of Cyrene" who, even if they do not yet have the faith, generously come to relieve your sufferings in your brothers and sisters.

When we come to the aid of our brethren in the persecuted Church, make us mindful that in reality it is we who, to an even greater extent, are being helped by them.

All:

Our Father, who art in heaven,
hallowed be thy name.
Thy Kingdom come.
Thy will be done on earth as it is in heaven.
Give us this day our daily bread,
and forgive us our trespasses,
as we forgive those who trespass against us,
and lead us not into temptation,
but deliver us from evil.

Let me share with You His pain,
Who for all my sins was slain,
Who for me in torments died.

Way of the Cross - 20th Century
Society of the Divine Word Generalate Archives - Rome

Ninth Station

Jesus meets the women of Jerusalem

V. *(genuflecting)* We adore you, O Christ and praise you.
R. Because by Your Holy Cross you have redeemed the world.

From the Gospel according to Luke 23:27-28

And there followed him a great multitude of the people, and of women who bewailed and lamented him. But Jesus turning to them said, "Daughters of Jerusalem, do not weep for me, but weep for yourselves and for your children."

Meditation

Women, especially mothers, derive from their love an immense capacity for endurance in suffering. They suffer through the actions of men, they suffer for their children. Let us think of the mothers of all those young people who are persecuted and imprisoned in the name of Christ. How many long nights those mothers spend awake and in tears! Let us think of the mothers who risk arrest and persecution as they persevere in family prayer, nourishing in their hearts the hope of better times ahead.

Prayer

Jesus, despite your sufferings, you were anxious to speak to the women along the Way of the Cross; make your consoling and enlightening voice heard today by so many suffering women.

You urge them not to weep for you, but for themselves and for their children.

Weeping over you, they weep over sufferings that bring salvation to humanity, and are therefore a cause of joy. What they should weep for, though, are the sufferings due to sin, which make them and their children and all of us like dry wood, worthy only to be tossed onto the fire.

Lord, you sent your Mother to repeat this same message to us at Lourdes and at Fatima: "Do penance and pray that the wrath of God may be halted." Move us at our final hour to accept this urgent appeal with sincere hearts!

All:

Our Father, who art in heaven,
hallowed be thy name.
Thy Kingdom come.
Thy will be done on earth as it is in heaven.
Give us this day our daily bread,
and forgive us our trespasses,
as we forgive those who trespass against us,
and lead us not into temptation,
but deliver us from evil.

O thou Mother! fount of love!
Touch my spirit from above.
Make my heart with Yours accord.

Way of the Cross - 20th Century
Society of the Divine Word Generalate Archives - Rome

Tenth Station

Jesus is crucified

V. *(genuflecting)* We adore you, O Christ and praise you.
R. Because by Your Holy Cross you have redeemed the world.

From the Gospel according to Mark 15:25, 31, 34

And it was the third hour when they crucified Jesus. The chief priests mocked him to one another with the scribes, saying, "He saved others, he cannot save himself." And at the ninth hour, Jesus cried with a loud voice, "My God, my God, why have you forsaken me?"

Meditation

Jesus, stripped of his garments, nailed to the cross, prey to untold sufferings, mocked by his enemies, feels abandoned even by the Father. This is the hell deserved by our sins. Jesus remained on the cross, he did not save himself.

In him were fulfilled the prophecies of the Suffering Servant: "He had no form or comeliness... no beauty... we esteemed him stricken, smitten by God... all we like sheep have gone astray; we have turned every one to his own way; and the Lord has laid on him the iniquity of us all. He was oppressed, and he was afflicted, yet he opened not his mouth; like a lamb that is led to the slaughter, and like a sheep that before its shearers is dumb" (*Is* 53:2, 4, 6-7).

Prayer

O Crucified Jesus, not only on Tabor, but even more on Calvary you revealed to us your true face, the face of a love that endures to the end.

Sometimes, out of reverence, you are represented wearing a royal cloak even on the cross. But we are not afraid to show you to the world just as you were, hanging upon the gibbet that Friday, from the sixth hour until the ninth hour.

As we contemplate you on the cross, we are filled with shame over our unfaithfulness and with gratitude for your infinite mercy. O Lord, how much your love for us has cost you!

Putting our trust in the power that comes from your Passion, we promise never more to offend you. We wish one day to have the honour of being placed upon the cross ourselves, like Peter and Andrew. We are encouraged by the serenity and the joy that it has been granted us to see on the faces of your faithful servants, the martyrs of our age.

All:

Our Father, who art in heaven,
hallowed be thy name.
Thy Kingdom come.
Thy will be done on earth as it is in heaven.
Give us this day our daily bread,
and forgive us our trespasses,
as we forgive those who trespass against us,
and lead us not into temptation,
but deliver us from evil.

Make me feel as You have felt;
Make my soul to glow and melt,
With the love of Christ my Lord.

Way of the Cross - 20th Century
Society of the Divine Word Generalate Archives - Rome

Eleventh Station

Jesus promises his Kingdom to the Good Thief

V. *(genuflecting)* We adore you, O Christ and praise you.
R. Because by Your Holy Cross you have redeemed the world.

From the Gospel according to Luke 23:33, 42-43

And when they came to the place which is called The Skull, there they crucified Jesus, and the criminals, one on the right and one on the left. One of the criminals said, "Jesus, remember me when you come into your kingdom." And he said to him, "Truly, I say to you, today you will be with me in Paradise."

Meditation

He was an evil-doer. He represents all evil-doers, that is to say, all of us. He had the good fortune to be close to Jesus in suffering, but all of us have this good fortune. Like him, let us say: "Lord, remember us when you come into your kingdom." We will receive the same reply.

And what of those who do not have the good fortune to be close to Jesus? Jesus is close to them, to each and every one.

"Jesus, remember us": let us speak these words to him for ourselves, for our friends, for our enemies and for the persecutors of our friends. The salvation of all people is the Lord's true victory.

Prayer

Jesus, remember me when, conscious of my unfaithfulness, I am tempted to despair.

Jesus, remember me when, after repeated efforts, I once more find myself deep in the valley of darkness.

Jesus, remember me when everyone is weary of me and no one trusts me anymore, and I find myself alone and abandoned.

All:
Our Father, who art in heaven,
hallowed be thy name.
Thy Kingdom come.
Thy will be done on earth as it is in heaven.
Give us this day our daily bread,
and forgive us our trespasses,
as we forgive those who trespass against us,
and lead us not into temptation,
but deliver us from evil.

Holy Mother! pierce me through;
In my heart each wound renew,
Of my Saviour crucified.

Way of the Cross - 20th Century
Society of the Divine Word Generalate Archives - Rome

Twelfth Station

The Mother of Jesus and the beloved disciple
at the foot of the Cross

V. *(genuflecting)* We adore you, O Christ and praise you.
R. Because by Your Holy Cross you have redeemed
the world.

From the Gospel according to John 19:25-27

*Standing by the Cross of Jesus were his mother, and his
mother's sister, Mary the wife of Clopas, and Mary
Magdalene. When Jesus saw his mother, and the disciple
whom he loved standing near, he said to his mother,
"Woman, behold your son!" Then he said to the disciple,
"Behold your mother!" And from that hour the disciple
took her to his own home.*

Meditation

Jesus is not thinking of himself even in that moment of
supreme suffering: he thinks of his Mother and he thinks
of us. Does he first of all entrust his Mother to the
disciple, as St John seems to suggest, or does he rather
entrust the disciple to his Mother?

Be that as it may, for the disciple, Mary will always be
the Mother entrusted to him by his dying Master, and for

Mary the disciple will always be the son entrusted to her by her dying Son; she will remain spiritually close to him, especially at the hour of death. Alongside all dying martyrs, then, she, their Mother, will always be standing at the foot of their cross, supporting them.

Prayer

Jesus and Mary, you shared suffering even to the end: Jesus on the cross, and Mary at the foot of the cross. A spear pierced the Saviour's side and a sword penetrated the heart of the Virgin Mother.

In truth, it is we through our sins who have caused such suffering.

Accept the repentance of us all, since through our weakness we have always been exposed to the risk of betraying, denying and deserting.

Accept the homage of faithfulness from all those who have followed the example of St John, who remained courageously at the foot of the Cross.

Jesus and Mary, I give you my heart and my soul. Jesus and Mary, help me in my final agony. Jesus and Mary, may my last breath be at peace with you.

All:

Our Father, who art in heaven,
hallowed be thy name.
Thy Kingdom come.
Thy will be done on earth as it is in heaven.
Give us this day our daily bread,
and forgive us our trespasses,
as we forgive those who trespass against us,
and lead us not into temptation,
but deliver us from evil.

Let me mingle tears with You,
Mourning Him who mourned for me,
All the days that I may live.

Way of the Cross - 20th Century
Society of the Divine Word Generalate Archives - Rome

Thirteenth Station

Jesus dies on the Cross

V. *(genuflecting)* We adore you, O Christ and praise you.
R. Because by Your Holy Cross you have redeemed the world.

From the Gospel according to Luke 23:46

Jesus, crying with a loud voice, said, "Father, into your hands I commit my spirit!" And having said this, he breathed his last.

Meditation

Jesus truly dies, because he is truly man. He hands over his last breath to the Father. O, how precious is that breath! The breath of life was given to the first man, and it is given to us once more, in a new way, after the Resurrection of Jesus, so that we are able to offer every breath to him who gave us breath. What fear we have of death and how enslaved we are by this fear! The meaning and value of a life are determined by the manner in which it is given away. Even for the unbeliever it is not acceptable to cling to life, losing all sense of its meaning. And for Jesus, there is no greater love than that which leads us to lay down our life for our friends. Those who are attached to life will lose it. Those who are ready to sacrifice it will keep it.

The martyrs give the supreme testimony of their love. They are not ashamed of their Master before men. The Master will be proud of them before all humanity on the last day.

Prayer

Jesus, you assumed human life so that you could give it away. In taking on our sinful human flesh, you, immortal King, became mortal. In accepting the most tragic and dark death, the ultimate fruit of sin, you accomplished the supreme act of complete trust in the Father. *In manus tuas, Domine, commendo spiritum meum.*

All:
Our Father, who art in heaven,
hallowed be thy name.
Thy Kingdom come.
Thy will be done on earth as it is in heaven.
Give us this day our daily bread,
and forgive us our trespasses,
as we forgive those who trespass against us,
and lead us not into temptation,
but deliver us from evil.

For the sins of His own nation,
Saw Him hang in desolation,
Till His spirit forth He sent.

Way of the Cross - 20th Century
Society of the Divine Word Generalate Archives - Rome

Fourteenth Station

*Jesus is taken down from the Cross
and placed in the tomb*

V. *(genuflecting)* We adore you, O Christ and praise you.
R. Because by Your Holy Cross you have redeemed
the world.

From the Gospel according to Mark 15:46
*Joseph of Arimathea bought a linen shroud, and taking
the body of Jesus down from the Cross, wrapped him in
the linen shroud, and laid him in a tomb which had been
hewn out of the rock. And he rolled a stone against the
door of the tomb.*

Meditation

Jesus chose not to come down alive from the Cross, but
to rise from the tomb. True death, true silence, the
Word of Life will be silent for three days.

Let us imagine the shock experienced by our first
parents upon seeing the lifeless body of Abel, the first
victim of death.

Let us think of Mary's sorrow as she embraces the
body of Jesus, now reduced to a heap of wounds, more a
worm than a man, no longer capable of returning his

Mother's loving gaze. Now she must consign him to the cold stones of the tomb, after hastily washing him and laying him out. It only remains now to wait. How interminable that wait seems, until the third day.

Prayer

Lord, the three days seem so long to us. Our stronger brethren grow weary, our weaker brethren gradually sink lower and lower, while the arrogant hold their heads high. Give perseverance to the strong, Lord, rouse the weak, and lead the hearts of all to conversion.

Are we right to be in a hurry, to want to see the victory of the Church straight away? Does our victory not consist rather in our eagerness to see it? Lord, grant us the perseverance to stand alongside the Church of silence and to accept that we will disappear and die like the grain of wheat.

Help us always to be mindful of your words, Lord: "Do not be afraid! I have overcome the world. I shall never fail you. I am with you always, until the end of the world."

Lord, increase our faith!

All·
Our Father, who art in heaven,
hallowed be thy name.
Thy Kingdom come.
Thy will be done on earth as it is in heaven.
Give us this day our daily bread,
and forgive us our trespasses,
as we forgive those who trespass against us,
and lead us not into temptation,
but deliver us from evil.

While the body here decays,
May my soul Thy goodness praise,
Safe in paradise with Thee. Amen.

Via Crucis

This year we have also walked along the Way of the Cross, the *Via Crucis*, evoking again with faith the stages of Christ's Passion. Our eyes have seen again the sufferings and anguish that our Redeemer had to bear in the hour of great sorrow, which marked the climax of his earthly mission.

Jesus dies on the Cross and lies in the tomb. The day of Good Friday, so permeated by human sadness and religious silence, closes in the silence of meditation and prayer. In returning home, we too, like those who were present at the sacrifice of Jesus, "beat our breasts", recalling what happened (cf. *Lk* 23:48). Is it possible to remain indifferent before the death of God? For us, for our salvation he became man and died on the Cross.

Brothers and sisters, our gaze is frequently distracted by scattered and passing earthly interests; let us direct our gaze today toward Christ. Let us pause to contemplate his Cross. The Cross is the source of immortal life, the school of justice and peace, the universal patrimony of pardon and mercy. It is permanent proof of an oblative and infinite love that brought God to become man, vulnerable like us, even to dying crucified. His nailed arms are open to each human being and they invite us to draw near to him, certain that he accepts us and clasps us in an embrace of infinite tenderness: "I, when I am lifted up from the earth, will draw all men to myself" (*Jn* 12:32).

Through the sorrowful Way of the Cross, the men and women of all ages, reconciled and redeemed by Christ's blood, have become friends of God, sons and daughters of the Heavenly Father. "Friend" is what Jesus calls Judas and he offers him the last and dramatic call to conversion. He calls each of us friend because he is the true friend of everyone. Unfortunately, we do not always manage to perceive the depth of this limitless love that God has for his creatures. For him there is no distinction of race or culture. Jesus Christ died to liberate the whole of humanity from ignorance of God, from the circle of hate and vengeance, from the slavery to sin. The Cross makes us brothers and sisters.

Let us ask ourselves: but what have we done with this gift? What have we done with the revelation of the Face of God in Christ, with the revelation of God's love that conquers hate. Many, in our age as well, do not know God and cannot find him in the crucified Christ. Many are in search of a love or a liberty that excludes God. Many believe they have no need of God. Dear friends: After having lived together Jesus' Passion, let us this evening allow his sacrifice on the cross to question us.

Let us permit him to put our human certainties in crisis. Let us open our hearts to him. Jesus is the truth that makes us free to love. Let us not be afraid: upon dying, the Lord saved sinners, that is, all of us. The Apostle Peter wrote: Jesus "himself bore our sins in his body upon the cross, that we might die to sin and live to righteousness. By his wounds you have been healed" (1 *Pt* 2: 24). This is the truth of Good Friday: on the cross, the Redeemer has restored to us the dignity that belongs to us, has made us adoptive sons and daughters of God whom he has created in his image and likeness. Let us remain, then, in adoration before the cross. O Christ, crucified King, give us true knowledge of you, the joy for which we yearn, the love that fills our heart, thirsty for the infinite. This is our prayer for this evening, Jesus, Son of God, who died for us on the cross and was raised up on the third day. Amen.

Way of the Cross at the Colosseum.
Address of His Holiness Benedict XVI
Good Friday, 21st March 2008.